the elegant
olive

TERESA KENNEDY

COOK WEST
S E R I E S

RIO NUEVO PUBLISHERS
TUCSON, ARIZONA

contents

xxxxxx

The world's love affair with the olive has been going on since prehistoric times. First cultivated in Asia Minor as early as 6000 B.C., wild olive shoots were propagated and spread all over the world.

The grandmother of all olive varieties is *Olea europaea*, a member of the same botanic family as jasmine and lilac. Close relations include certain varieties of ash trees and a number of other hardwoods. It wasn't long before the noble and elegant fruit began to acquire sacred significance. The Greeks and Egyptians not only cultivated these trees, but revered them. But it was the Greeks who raised the olive and its oil to a place in their culture unparalleled by any other material, food, or plant.

In Greek mythology, the olive tree is closely associated with the goddess Athena. According to legend, the olive was the goddess of wisdom's gift to mankind—a tree that gives light, fruit and delicious oil, shade for rest, and a very valuable wood. To honor Athena, an orchard—the City of Olive—was planted on top of the Acropolis. The orchard regenerated itself after the invading Persians set it on fire. In life as in legend, the olive tree is very nearly indestructible and will regenerate itself whenever it is damaged. It's reported that some trees are still producing fruit after twenty-three hundred years!

Over time, the olive and its oil served as inspiration to the great civilizations of the world. The graceful olive branch was selected as a universal sign of peace, while selected olive oils have at various times been considered as valuable as gold, traded in opulent, highly decorated urns and jars or finely wrought Roman vases.

All three of the major religions that spring from the Mediterranean area—Judaism, Islam, and Christianity—give olive oil a sacred place in anointing ceremonies. The Greek word chrism means "to anoint with oil" and is the derivation of the word "Christ."

In the Middle East, the story is told of Adam suffering from pain and complaining to God. At that, Gabriel descended from heaven with an olive tree, presented it to Adam, and said, "Plant it, then pick the fruit and press out its oil. It will cure your pain and all sickness." In the Bible, olive oil is recommended to "make him a cheerful countenance," right along with "wine that maketh glad the heart of man." Thus, early Middle Eastern cultures believed it would cure every illness except death. To this day, many people around the world drink half a cup of olive oil before breakfast to keep their systems well lubricated.

It is easier to understand the olive's importance to early cultures once we understand just how much the olive offers. Its fruit supplied food, medicine, and even light when the oil was used as fuel. The leaves provided fodder for livestock. In summer, the trees gave shade and shelter, and in winter, firewood. Little wonder that a tree with so many vital uses was thought to be a gift from the gods.

In the New World, the first olive trees were planted in California around 1769 by Franciscan missionaries. In fact, all the "Mission olives" grown today in California probably derive from trees grown at the first Franciscan missions in California. Today olives are commercially grown in Spain, Italy, France, Greece, Tunisia, Morocco, Turkey, Portugal, China, Chile, Peru, Brazil, Mexico, Angola, South Africa, Uruguay, Afghanistan, Australia, New Zealand, California, and most recently, Texas. And the popularity of both olives and olive oil only continues to soar. In the United States, olive oil imports rose 15.4 percent per year from 1981 to 1991 and another 100 percent from 1991 to 2003. And when you consider that it takes about a ton of olives to produce just 50 gallons of olive oil—that's a lot of olives!

Rich in antioxidants and monounsaturated fats, olives and their oils are thought to help fight potential heart disease, ulcers, gallstones, and colon cancer. Olive oil is also thought to lower "bad" cholesterol levels in the blood.

OLIVE VARIETIES

My own love affair with the olive began with a little Italian grocery store in the town where I grew up. Like any kid, I was reluctant to try the mysterious, oily-looking things my parents seemed so fond of, but once I did, I was hooked. From then on, I loved them all—black and wrinkly, green with specks of red pepper, purple, yellow, and gold. Italian, Spanish, Greek, French, or Californian—there was a whole world of olives out there, and I couldn't wait to try them.

So why are olives different colors? Most of the time, it's not so much a difference in variety as a difference in size, ripeness, and curing method. While many olive growers make much of one variety or another, the fact is that all varietals require some form of cross-pollination to produce fruit and all are related in some form to the *Olea europaea*.

All fresh olives are bitter and tough—whether they're unripe and green, any shade of getting-ripe and red to purplish, or fully ripe and black. So, at harvest, they have to be separated according to color and size, cured in salt, lye, or wood ash, then cured again in either dry salt, wet salt (brine), and/or oil—or dry roasted. Finally, the olives are packed in either oil, vinegar, or a marinade flavored with herbs and spices.

The world catalog of olive varieties currently lists more than 130 cultivars, and each country has its own unique varieties planted for both table olives and oil production. With the olive's increasing popularity, many of these have become well known amongst olive lovers and epicures everywhere.

Greece is most famous for its Kalamata varietal, which is cured with brine to a rich purple. In France, we find the Niçoise, which is smaller, red-brown, and lightly salted. Also from France are the Picholines—tiny, pointed olives with a tangy fruit flavor, typically marinated with citrus and *herbes des Provence.*

Italy abounds with olive varieties, and some groves there are indeed so old it's nearly impossible to tell which varieties were originally planted. Popular types include Frantonio, Leccino, and Picual, which are all prized for their oil, while further south in Sicily, the favored varieties include Carolea, Nocellara, and Biancolilla. Spain runs a close second to Italy in olive and olive oil production and currently dominates in world production of table olives with Manzanillo, Sevillano, and Ascolano.

In California, Manzanillo and Sevillano make up about 90 percent of the olive harvest, along with small amounts of Mission, Ascolano, and others. Sevillanos are twice the size of Manzanillos, but their low oil content makes them suitable for use only as a table olive. Mission olives were formerly the most popular variety grown in California, but small fruit size, relatively large stones, and susceptibility to diseases and frost led to their decline in popularity.

Arbequino Sweet and fruity olives from Spain; small and greenish brown in color.

Calabrese Tannish green olives grown around Calabria, Italy, often cured with fennel.

Gaeta Italian olives with a sharp flavor and soft, chewy texture.

Kalamata Greek olives, brine-cured to a rich purple color; these are popular imported olives.

Mission Mostly grown in California, these olives are picked green but turn black during the curing process.

Niçoise Small reddish-brown olives from France, with a nutty rich flavor.

Picholine Small, tart, and slightly smoky olives from France.

Sicilian Typically grown in California, these olives are tangy, crunchy, and salty.

Spanish Young green olives, usually cured first in lye then fermented in brine. Queens and Manzanillas are two common types, and Spanish olives are also often stuffed.

Stuffed olives After pitting, olives may be filled with garlic, pimientos, jalapeños, almonds, anchovies, blue cheese, or almost anything that will fit.

Artichoke and Olive Tapenade

xxxxxx

Most often served with fresh veggies as a dip or with toasted bread as an appetizer, this versatile tapenade also makes an excellent sauce for grilled fish.

Place the garlic and anchovies in the workbowl of a food processor. Pulse to a paste.

In a separate bowl, combine the olives, artichoke hearts, garlic and anchovy paste, capers, lemon juice and zest, orange juice and zest, olive oil, and parsley. Add salt and pepper to taste.

Refrigerate for at least 30 minutes before serving, to allow the flavors to develop. Tapenade will keep for up to 2 weeks in the refrigerator.

Makes about 3 cups

3 cloves garlic, peeled

3 anchovies

1/2 cup pitted black ripe olives, chopped

1/2 cup pitted green olives, chopped

1 cup canned artichoke hearts (about 10), drained and sliced

3 tablespoons capers, rinsed

Zest and juice of 1 small lemon

Zest and juice of 1 small orange

1/3 cup extra-virgin olive oil

1/3 cup chopped fresh Italian parsley

Salt and fresh pepper

Tapenade Provençal

xxxxxx

Makes about 1 cup

1/2 cup basil leaves, rinsed

1/3 cup pitted
Kalamata olives

1/3 cup pitted small green
olives such as Picholine

2 cloves garlic, peeled

1 tablespoon
drained capers

2 sun-dried tomato halves

4 flat anchovy
fillets, drained

1/4 cup extra-virgin olive oil

2 tablespoons mayonnaise

Juice and zest of 1 lemon

Here is a more traditional tapenade, rich with the sultry flavors of the Mediterranean. Though it's always a favorite as a dip with crudités or breads, it's also especially good over pasta.

Combine the basil, olives, garlic, capers, tomatoes, and anchovies in the workbowl of a food processor. Pulse lightly until ingredients are well blended and minced thoroughly. Add the olive oil, mayonnaise, lemon juice, and zest. Process to a smooth paste. Remove to a serving bowl and chill.

Serve with assorted vegetables or breads as a dip.

Fried Olives

xxxxxx

Though this can seem time-consuming, the scrumptious results will have you adding this indispensable recipe to your repertoire. Keep in mind that this recipe is easily doubled, and breaded olives can be frozen to fry up later on.

Remove the sausage meat from its casing and place it in a medium bowl. Add the garlic, a pinch of salt, and red pepper flakes, if desired. Mix well.

Drain the olives and rinse them under cold water. Stuff each of the olives with ¼ to ½ teaspoon of the sausage mixture.

Heat the oil in a deep fryer, or stockpot, to 375 degrees F. Spread the flour on a dinner plate. Break the eggs into a shallow bowl and beat lightly. Spread the bread crumbs on another dinner plate and sprinkle them with salt and pepper. Moisten the olives with the olive oil, stirring to evenly distribute the flavors.

Roll the olives in the flour, dip them in egg, and roll in bread crumbs. Fry the olives until golden brown and the sausage in the middle is cooked through, about 3 minutes. Drain on paper towels to absorb any excess oil. Serve warm or at room temperature.

Makes 6 appetizer portions

¼ **pound (1 link) fresh Italian sausage**

1 **teaspoon minced garlic**

Pinch of salt

½ **teaspoon crushed red pepper flakes (optional)**

1 **jar (8 ounces) large pitted green olives, drained**

3 **cups vegetable oil, for deep-frying**

½ **cup all-purpose flour**

2 **large eggs**

½ **cup seasoned bread crumbs**

Salt and freshly ground pepper

2 **teaspoons extra-virgin olive oil**

Citrus-Marinated Olives

xxxxxx

Makes about 3 cups

1 1/2 cups Kalamata or other brine-cured black olives

1 1/2 cups cracked brine-cured green olives

1 cup olive oil

1/4 cup chopped fresh cilantro

1/4 cup fresh lemon juice

1/4 cup orange juice

6 large garlic cloves, thinly sliced

3 tablespoons chopped fresh parsley

1 tablespoon grated lemon zest

1 tablespoon grated orange zest

1/2 teaspoon dried crushed red pepper

Marinating brined olives can add a number of wonderful and subtle variations to the olive's noble flavor—don't be afraid to experiment!

Combine all ingredients in a large, resealable plastic bag. Shake bag to blend ingredients.

Refrigerate at least 1 day and up to 3 days, turning bag occasionally. Transfer olives and some marinade to bowl. Let stand 1 hour at room temperature before serving.

Variations For Chile Olives, substitute 3 or 4 dried red chile peppers for the grated lemon and lime zest, then mix and marinate as directed. For Herbed Olives, substitute 2 or 3 sprigs fresh rosemary for the cilantro; eliminate the orange juice and add 1/2 cup shredded basil leaves and 1 bay leaf; proceed as above. For North African Olives, substitute oil-cured black olives for Kalamata olives; eliminate orange juice and orange zest; add 2 or 3 dried red chile peppers, a generous teaspoon of ground cumin, and 1 bay leaf, and proceed as above.

Tomato and Olive Salsa

xxxxxx

A new twist on an old favorite. The marvel here is that it strikes a perfect balance between the mellow flavor of olives and the tanginess of fresh tomatoes.

In the workbowl of a food processor, lightly chop the tomatoes. Add the garlic, onion, olives, peppers, lime, olive oil, and salt and pepper. Pulse lightly. Transfer to a serving bowl. Stir in the Tabasco sauce as desired. Serve at room temperature with tortilla chips.

Makes 2 cups

3–4 tomatoes, seeded

2 cloves garlic, minced

$1/2$ medium sweet onion

$1/2$ cup pitted and chopped Kalamata olives

$1/2$ cup mixed assorted bell peppers (green, gold, or red)

Juice and zest of 1 lime or to taste

2 tablespoons extra-virgin olive oil

Salt and pepper

Dash of Tabasco sauce

Pimiento Olive and Cheese Canapés

xxxxxx

This spread is a far cry from the bright-orange gook often found in your supermarket's dairy case. Olives add a special texture and flavor to an old appetizing favorite.

Preheat oven to broil. Combine all ingredients except bread in a medium-size bowl. Mix well.

Spread half of the mixture on each portion of the bread. Place bread, face up, under broiler and broil 3–5 minutes or until cheese is melted and slightly browned.

Slice into 2-inch slices, arrange on a platter, and serve warm.

Serves 12 as an appetizer

10 ounces sharp Cheddar cheese, grated

1 package cream cheese (8 ounces), softened

$1/2$ cup minced onion

$1/2$ cup chili sauce

$1/4$ cup sliced pimiento-stuffed olives

$1/4$ cup sour cream

1 loaf crusty French bread, sliced in half horizontally

Olive Tomato Squares

XXXXXX

Makes 24
hors d'oeuvres

1/4 cup prepared basil pesto

6 slices firm white sandwich
bread, crusts discarded

1/3 cup pitted Kalamata
olives, slivered

1/4 cup drained and
chopped oil-packed
sun-dried tomatoes

1 tablespoon chopped fresh
Italian parsley or cilantro

An easy and elegant offering for cocktails or parties.

Place oven rack in middle position and preheat oven to 400 degrees F.

Spread 2 teaspoons of pesto evenly on each slice of bread, then quarter each slice. Toast the bread squares on a baking sheet until undersides are golden, about 10 minutes.

Meanwhile, soak the olives and tomatoes in warm water to cover for 5 minutes, then drain well, pressing out excess moisture, and toss with parsley or cilantro. Mound onto the prepared toasts and serve.

Olives Baked in Red Wine

XXXXXX

Makes about 1 cup

1 cup unpitted
Kalamata olives or other
brine-cured black olives

1/2 cup dry red wine

1/2 teaspoon fennel seeds,
lightly crushed

1 sprig fresh rosemary,
lightly bruised

1 large clove garlic, peeled
and thinly sliced

2 teaspoons
extra-virgin olive oil

Here, the briny, robust flavor of Kalamata olives is softened and sweetened with wine and fennel. As always when cooking with wine, the better the wine, the better the flavor.

Preheat oven to 325 degrees F. Combine olives, wine, fennel seeds, rosemary, garlic, and olive oil in small baking dish. Bake uncovered until olives are heated through, about 20 minutes. Cool slightly. Serve olives warm, garnished with additional rosemary as desired.

Baked Cheddar Olives

xxxxxx

*Makes about 24
Cheddar olives*

1 cup grated
sharp Cheddar cheese

2 tablespoons
unsalted butter, softened

$1/2$ cup all-purpose flour

$1/8$ teaspoon cayenne pepper

1 jar (3 ounces) small
pimiento-stuffed
green olives (about 24),
drained and patted dry

Make these for a party and they'll disappear by the handful!

Preheat oven to 400 degrees F. In a bowl, combine the Cheddar and butter, add flour and cayenne, and blend the dough until it is combined well. Drop the dough by tablespoons onto wax paper, and wrap or mold each tablespoon around each of the olives, covering each olive completely.

Bake the wrapped olives on a baking sheet in the middle of the oven for 15 minutes, or until the pastry is golden, and serve them warm.

Roasted Olives with Fennel and Lemons

xxxxxx

Serves 8

8 ounces imported black
olives such as Kalamata

4 garlic cloves,
peeled and sliced

$1/2$ lemon, scrubbed
and thinly sliced

$1/4$ cup extra-virgin olive oil

1 teaspoon fennel seeds

Pinch of crushed red pepper

People of the Mediterranean know that citrus and olives make for a near-perfect marriage of flavors—the fennel seed in this recipe insures that it is indeed a marriage made in heaven!

Preheat oven to 350 degrees F. In an 8-inch baking pan, spread the olives, garlic, and lemon. Drizzle with the olive oil and sprinkle with fennel seeds and red pepper. Bake for 45 minutes, stirring the olives at least 3 times.

Remove from oven and store in the refrigerator. Keeps for up to a month.

Olive-and-Anchovy–Stuffed Eggs

xxxxxx

A fabulous and unusual choice for brunch, or great as an appetizer, too!

Halve eggs crosswise and scoop out yolks into the workbowl of a food processor. Combine the yolks with the sour cream, minced olives, anchovies, vinegar, salt and pepper, and minced Italian parsley. Pulse lightly until very smooth.

Spoon or pipe mounds of filling into the egg-white halves. Garnish with additional olives and parsley. Chill at least 2 hours before serving.

Makes 12 stuffed eggs

6 large hard-boiled eggs

3 tablespoons sour cream

6 Kalamata or other brine-cured black olives, pitted and minced

6 flat anchovy fillets, drained and minced

1 teaspoon white wine vinegar

Salt and pepper

2–3 tablespoons minced fresh Italian parsley

Black olive slivers, for garnish

Additional Italian chopped parsley, for garnish

Pesto, Olive, and Roasted-Pepper Goat Cheese Torta

xxxxxx

Makes 1 loaf,
approximately 12
appetizer portions

¼ cup prepared basil pesto

Vegetable oil for the pan

¼ cup finely chopped
roasted red bell peppers,
rinsed and drained

20 ounces mild goat
cheese, softened at room
temperature (about 2 cups)

3 tablespoons bottled black
olive paste or Tapenade
Provençal (see page 14)

Special equipment:
2¼-cup loaf pan
(5³/4 x 3¹/2 x 2 ¹/4 inches)

A beautiful and elegant no-cook appetizer.

Drain pesto in a small fine-mesh sieve for 15 minutes, lightly pressing out the excess oil. Lightly oil the loaf pan and line it with a sheet of plastic wrap large enough to allow a generous overhang on all 4 sides. Blot the peppers well between paper towels to remove excess liquid.

Spread about ¼ of the cheese evenly over the bottom of the pan; then spread the pesto over it. Drop ½ cup of the cheese by tablespoons over the pesto and spread evenly to cover. Top with chopped peppers, spreading evenly. Drop another ½ cup of cheese by tablespoons over the peppers and spread gently to cover. Spread olive paste or tapenade evenly on top, then drop the remaining cheese by tablespoons over the olive paste, spreading gently to cover. Cover the pan with another sheet of plastic wrap and chill at least 8 hours.

Remove plastic wrap from top of pan and invert torta onto a serving plate, then peel off remaining plastic wrap. The torta can be chilled in the pan up to 24 hours. Let the torta stand at room temperature 20 minutes before serving.

Salads
xxxxxx

Fennel, Olive, and Blood Orange Salad

xxxxxx

This is a wonderful wintertime salad. The flavors are all strong and fresh.

Trim the tops and any bruised outer leaves from the fennel. Cut in half lengthwise and slice thinly (a mandolin works well here, but watch the fingers). Toss with lemon juice.

In a small bowl whisk together the orange juice, olive oil, and salt and pepper.

Combine the fennel, mesclun salad mix, orange segments, olives, and parsley leaves in a serving bowl. Toss gently with the vinaigrette. Shave the Parmesan over the top and serve.

Serves 6

3 fennel bulbs

1 lemon, juiced

Juice of 1 orange

$1/3$ cup extra-virgin olive oil

Salt and pepper

2 cups mesclun salad mix

2 blood oranges, segmented

$1/3$ cup pitted olives

$1/2$ cup Italian parsley leaves

$1/4$ pound Parmesan cheese

Salade Niçoise

xxxxxx

Serves 4–6

This classic favorite French dressing is absolutely delicious for a dinner or luncheon salad served with crusty French bread.

¼ cup mayonnaise

¼ cup crème fraîche

1 shallot, peeled and chopped

20 green olives, pitted and chopped (use a smaller variety, such as Picholine)

½ cup small capers, rinsed

4 fillets of anchovy, drained and chopped

1 tablespoon Dijon mustard

Juice of half a lemon

Extra-virgin olive oil

Salt and pepper

8–10 tiny red-skinned potatoes

1 pound thin, tender green beans (*haricots verts*)

1 tablespoon olive oil

3 tomatoes, each cut into 6 wedges

6 hard-boiled eggs, chilled and cut into wedges

2 bell peppers, any color, cut into thin strips

2 cans (7 ounces each) white albacore tuna, chilled and drained

1 bunch French Breakfast radishes, topped and sliced

1 head butter lettuce, torn

Prepare the dressing by whisking together the mayonnaise, crème fraîche, shallot, green olives, capers, anchovies, Dijon, lemon juice, olive oil, and salt and pepper to taste in a bowl until completely combined. Chill completely before preparing the salad.

Halve the potatoes and steam until tender. Set aside to cool. Cook the green beans in boiling salted water with olive oil, uncovered, for 3–5 minutes. Drain and chill.

To assemble the salad platter, arrange the various ingredients in mounds, placing 2 separate bundles of green beans at either end of the platter, tomato wedges all around, and the potatoes, eggs, peppers, tuna, and radishes in the center over the torn lettuce.

Whisk the dressing again until smooth, then drizzle over entire salad. Garnish with additional olives and anchovies.

Greek Salad
xxxxxx

Rich, robust, and completely satisfying, this classic favorite surely has thousands of variations. This, however, is simply one of the best.

For the dressing, combine the reserved anchovy oil and olive oil to equal ½ cup. In a jar, combine the oils, vinegar, bay leaf, garlic, and oregano. Shake well and chill several hours.

In a large salad bowl, combine the anchovy fillets, parsley, lettuce, onion, tomatoes, cucumber, bell pepper, olives, and feta cheese. Remove the bay leaf from the jar of dressing, shake dressing well, and pour over salad.

Serves 4–6

1 can anchovy fillets, drained (reserve oil)

Extra-virgin olive oil

¼ cup wine vinegar

1 bay leaf

1 clove garlic, peeled and bruised

1 teaspoon oregano

¼ cup chopped parsley

1 bunch romaine lettuce, torn into pieces

½ head of iceberg lettuce, torn into pieces

4 endive lettuce leaves, torn into pieces

2 red onions, thinly sliced

2 ripe tomatoes, cut into chunks

1 cucumber, scored and sliced

½ green bell pepper, cut in strips

12 Kalamata olives, pitted

¼–½ pound crumbled feta cheese

Olive and Potato Salad

xxxxxx

Serves 6

1 pound boiled potatoes, peeled and diced

2 boiled eggs, peeled and diced

2 medium tomatoes, diced

1/2 red bell pepper, diced

1/2 onion, diced

1 medium cucumber, diced

2 stalks celery, diced

1 tablespoon capers, drained

1/2 cup extra-large Kalamata olives

1 can (7 ounces) tuna (in water or oil)

2–3 tablespoons olive oil

2 tablespoons balsamic vinegar

1/2 tablespoon salt

A lovely change from the usual potato salad—great for picnics as it doesn't include mayonnaise, which can spoil easily, especially in warm weather.

Mix all ingredients together in a bowl, cover, and refrigerate. Serve at lunch or dinner as desired.

As Good As It Gets Olive Salad

xxxxxx

No refrigerator should be without it…as the salad marinates, feel free to keep adding ingredients of your own choice— pickled mushrooms, artichoke hearts, crumbled Gorgonzola— see for yourself just how good it can get!

Combine the bell pepper strips and olives and set aside.

In another bowl, whisk together the olive oil, vinegar, garlic, basil, red onion, cayenne, salt, and pepper. Pour the vinaigrette over the olive-pepper mixture and stir. Cover and refrigerate.

Makes about 2 cups

1 red bell pepper, cut into strips

20 large green olives, chopped

15 extra-large or colossal black olives, chopped

1 cup extra-virgin olive oil

$1/4$ cup balsamic vinegar

6 cloves fresh garlic, chopped, more or less

$1/4$ cup chopped fresh basil

$1/4$ cup chopped sweet red onion

Pinch of cayenne pepper

Salt

Freshly ground black pepper

Mushroom Custard in Roasted Onion with Arugula and Kalamata Vinaigrette

xxxxx

Serves 4

2 Spanish onions, peeled

4 ounces wild mushrooms

1 tablespoon olive oil (not extra-virgin)

1 tablespoon butter

1 shallot, chopped

1 teaspoon fresh thyme

1 cup heavy cream

2 eggs

Salt

10 Kalamata or Gaeta olives, pitted

1/8 cup red wine vinegar

3/4 cup extra-virgin olive oil

1 pound arugula

This recipe is a memorable combination of rich flavors that all come together with a wonderful subtlety. As you'll see from the instructions below, it's also much easier than the title would suggest, so don't be intimidated.

Preheat the oven to 300 degrees F. Place the onions in a pan of lightly salted cold water, and bring to a boil. Reduce heat and simmer until soft. Remove from the heat and reserve.

Sauté the mushrooms in olive oil and butter until most of the liquid has been absorbed. Add shallot and thyme, then continue to sauté for 2–3 minutes longer. Remove from the heat and chill.

Cut the onion tops and bottoms off, leaving about a fingertip-size hole. Remove the onion centers, leaving only 3 onion layers. Wrap the outer layer in plastic wrap, then foil. Leave the top part open to allow ventilation.

Mix cream, eggs, and a little salt. Fill each onion with the mushroom mixture, then pour in the cream and egg mixture. Bake the wrapped onions for 30 minutes, placing a small ramekin of water in the center of the tray to add moisture as the onions bake.

For the vinaigrette, chop the olives to a fine consistency, then add the vinegar and olive oil. Toss some of the vinaigrette with the arugula.

To serve, place a handful of the arugula salad in the center of a plate. Place the warm mushroom tart on top and drizzle vinaigrette around the plate.

Cannellini Bean Salad with Olives, Sun-dried Tomatoes, and Spinach

XXXXXX

Try this exciting variation on an old-time Tuscan favorite. Excellent for summer buffets, the salad is better made a day ahead and served chilled or at room temperature.

Heat the olive oil in a skillet over medium heat. Add the onion and sauté, stirring frequently, until slightly brown, about 5 minutes.

Toss the onion, beans, spinach, tomatoes, mozzarella, and olives in a large bowl with the vinaigrette until just combined. Season with salt and pepper. Serve immediately with grated Parmesan, or refrigerate in an airtight container until ready to use, reserving the Parmesan until ready to serve.

Variation   This recipe is very flexible. You can use orzo in place of the cannellini beans, as pictured here.

Serves 8–10

$1/4$ cup olive oil

1 yellow onion, finely chopped

2 cans (16 ounces each) cannellini beans, rinsed and drained

4 cups firmly packed spinach, washed, drained, and stems removed

1 cup chopped sun-dried tomatoes

$1/2$ pound fresh mozzarella cheese, cut into $1/2$-inch cubes

$1/2$ cup pitted black olives, such as Kalamata or Arbequino

1 cup Italian vinaigrette or bottled Italian salad dressing

Salt and freshly ground black pepper

$1/2$ cup grated Parmesan cheese

Spinach with Olives, Raisins, and Piñon Nuts

xxxxxx

Serves 6

Serve this either as a warmed salad or at room temperature. Marvelous.

2 packages (10 ounces each) ready-to-use fresh spinach leaves or 4 large bunches, rinsed and trimmed

$1/4$ cup olive oil

3 large garlic cloves, chopped

$1/3$ cup (generous) pitted brine-cured olives (such as Kalamata)

$1/3$ cup golden raisins

$1/4$ cup piñon nuts, toasted

$1 1/2$ tablespoons balsamic or red wine vinegar

Salt and pepper

Place a colander over a large bowl and line it with a kitchen towel. Wilt the spinach in a dry skillet over high heat about 3 minutes, stirring frequently. (Spinach should still be bright green.) Transfer the spinach to the prepared colander. Allow it to cool briefly, then gather the towel around the spinach and squeeze well, pressing out as much moisture as possible.

Heat the olive oil in a large heavy skillet over medium heat. Add the chopped garlic, olives, and raisins, and sauté until garlic begins to color, about 3 minutes. Add the spinach and toasted piñon nuts and toss until heated through. Add vinegar and toss again. Season generously with salt and pepper and serve.

Muffalatta Olive Salad

xxxxxx

1 cup slivered carrots

1 cup finely diced celery

1 cup finely diced
red sweet onions

1 cup chopped green olives

1 cup chopped black olives

1 cup chopped
fresh basil leaves

1/2 cup chopped peperoncini
(seeds and stems removed)

2 cups chopped bottled
roasted sweet red peppers,
liquid reserved

2 tablespoons
chopped garlic

1/4 cup Spanish capers

2 tablespoons
balsamic vinegar

2 tablespoons
granulated garlic

1 teaspoon white pepper

1 teaspoon black pepper

2 teaspoons oregano

1 teaspoon celery seed

1 teaspoon thyme

1 cup extra-virgin olive oil

This New Orleans tradition is a marinated mix that can be made and stored, covered, for up to 2 months in the refrigerator. Using a food processor to do the chopping makes preparation wonderfully simple. To make the legendary sandwiches from the Big Easy, refer to the recipe that follows.

Combine carrots, celery, and onions in a large bowl. Add the olives, basil, peperoncini, and roasted peppers, including the reserved liquid. Add the chopped garlic, capers, vinegar, granulated garlic, white pepper, black pepper, oregano, celery seed, thyme, and olive oil, and mix until well blended.

Place the salad in a plastic or glass container, cover tightly, and refrigerate. The salad may be used in 24 hours but kept no longer than 2 months.

MUFFALATTA OLIVE SALAD SANDWICH

Allow prepared Muffalatta Olive Salad (previous recipe) to stand overnight, refrigerated, so that flavors can mingle.

Slice the bread in half horizontally, scooping out some of the center of the loaf. Drizzle oil from the salad onto both halves of the bread. On the bottom half of the bread, layer the olive salad, cold cuts, and cheeses, and continue layering until all ingredients are used, and ending with a layer of onion slices. Put the top half of the bread back on and wrap tightly in foil or plastic wrap until ready to serve. Cut into 6 wedges and enjoy!

Serves 6

1 large, round loaf of bread

$1/3$ pound salami, thinly sliced

$1/3$ cup prosciutto or capicola ham, thinly sliced

$1/2$ pound provolone, thinly sliced

$1/2$ pound Havarti cheese, thinly sliced

$1/2$ red onion, sliced in circles

Red Pepper Fettuccine with Tuna and Olives

xxxxxx

A family favorite that can be put together in minutes. Definitely not your mother's tuna casserole!

In a large saucepan, sauté shallots and scallions in olive oil until translucent, about 2 minutes. Add basil, olives, tuna, lemon zest, and lemon juice. Season to taste with salt and pepper and stir until well heated. Set aside and cover to keep warm.

Meanwhile, bring a large pot of water to a rolling boil over high heat. Add pasta and 1 tablespoon salt and boil until al dente. Drain pasta and add to tuna-olive mixture. Toss well and briefly reheat before serving.

Serves 4

2 shallots, finely chopped

3 scallions with green tops, chopped

1/4 cup olive oil

12 large fresh basil leaves, finely shredded

20 pitted Kalamata olives

1 can tuna packed in olive oil

Zest of 1 lemon

2 teaspoons fresh lemon juice

Salt and freshly ground pepper

3/4 pound fresh or dried red pepper fettuccine

Orzo with Goat Cheese and Olives

XXXXXX

Serves 4

2 red bell peppers

2 yellow bell peppers

2 tablespoons olive oil, plus more for garnish

1/2 medium yellow onion, finely diced

12 ounces orzo

1/4 cup chopped oil-cured Kalamata olives, drained, plus more for garnish

3 ounces goat cheese, crumbled

Salt and freshly ground black pepper

1/4 cup fresh parsley leaves, for garnish

Orzo is a small, oval-shaped pasta traditionally used in soups and stews. Here, it's preferred simply because the pasta finishes cooking in the sauce and so absorbs more of the flavor.

Roast the peppers over the flame of a gas burner, on a hot grill, or under the broiler, until the skin is black and charred. Remove from heat and place in a large bowl. Cover with plastic wrap and allow to cool 15 to 20 minutes. With clean paper towels, wipe off the skin. Remove and discard the stems and seeds. If necessary, briefly rinse under cold water to remove any remaining charred skin. Dice the roasted peppers and set aside.

In a large pot, bring salted water to a boil. Meanwhile, heat a large sauté pan over medium-high heat. Add the olive oil. When the oil is hot, add the onion and cook just until translucent, but not browned, about 5 minutes. Add the reserved peppers and sauté for 3 minutes.

Blanch the orzo in the boiling water for 4 to 5 minutes, or until beginning to cook, but still very al dente. Drain, reserving the pasta water, and add orzo to the pepper mixture. Add 1 cup of the reserved pasta water and cook, stirring until the combination is creamy and the pasta is tender. Finish with another ¼ cup pasta water if the mixture is too thick.

Stir in the olives and goat cheese and mix until the cheese is melted. Season with salt and pepper, to taste. Thin with pasta water if the mixture is too thick. Garnish with parsley, olives, and a drizzle of olive oil.

Spaghetti with Olive Sauce

xxxxxx

As with all great Italian cooking, the success of this recipe depends on the freshness and simplicity of the ingredients. This sauce is so easy, you don't even have to cook it.

Combine olive oil, olives, onion, anchovies, parsley, garlic, orange zest, oregano, black pepper, and salt.

Cook the spaghetti in boiling water until al dente (7–10 minutes). Toss the spaghetti with room-temperature sauce. Serve with crusty French bread.

Serves 4–6 as a first or main course

$1/4$ cup olive oil

$1/4$ cup chopped pitted black olives

$1/4$ cup chopped mushroom-stuffed olives

$1/4$ cup chopped red onion

1 tablespoon drained and minced anchovies

1 tablespoon chopped Italian parsley

1 clove garlic, minced

1 teaspoon finely grated orange zest

$1/2$ teaspoon oregano

$1/4$ teaspoon coarsely ground black pepper

Salt

12 ounces spaghetti (or similar pasta)

Pasta with Green Olive and Celery Sauce

xxxxxx

Serves 2

Fresh, fast, and fabulous—this can also make the beginning of a great pasta salad.

¹/₂ cup habañero-stuffed olives, diced

¹/₂ cup diced celery

2 tablespoons chopped celery leaves

6 tablespoons olive oil

¹/₄ cup diced red onion

¹/₄ cup finely chopped parsley

1 clove garlic, crushed

¹/₄ teaspoon freshly ground black pepper

8 ounces small shell pasta, cooked and drained

Rinse the olives, drain them, and use paper towels to squeeze out extra moisture. Combine olives, celery, celery leaves, oil, onion, parsley, garlic, and pepper in a bowl. Toss the hot pasta with the sauce and serve warm—or serve chilled, if you prefer.

Linguine with Caramelized Onion, Bacon, and Olives

xxxxxx

One of the best late-night suppers I know. Serve with a robust, dry red wine.

Cook the bacon in a medium skillet until partially browned; drain off half the fat. Add olive oil and heat over low heat; add the onion and sauté until soft and the edges begin to turn golden, about 8 minutes. Add the garlic; sauté 1 minute. Stir in the olives.

Meanwhile, cook the linguine in plenty of boiling salted water until al dente, about 6 minutes; drain. Toss with the onion-bacon mixture, sage, and parsley, if using. Sprinkle with pepper and grated cheese.

Serves 4

12 strips bacon, cut into $1/2$-inch pieces

$1/2$ cup olive oil

2 onions, quartered and cut into thin lengthwise strips

4 cloves garlic, minced

$1/2$ cup imported black olives such as Kalamata or Arbequino, pitted and chopped

12 ounces linguine

1 tablespoon chopped fresh sage

4 tablespoons chopped fresh parsley (optional)

Coarsely ground black pepper

Grated Romano cheese

Rigatoni with Chunky Tomato and Green Olive Sauce

xxxxxx

Serves 4–6 as a first or main course

2 tablespoons olive oil

1/4 cup chopped onion

1 clove garlic, crushed

3 tablespoons chopped garlic-stuffed olives

1 can (28 ounces) whole plum tomatoes, with juice

1 tablespoon fresh basil, chopped

Salt and pepper

16 ounces rigatoni, cooked

For added zest, try adding 2 or 3 chopped anchovy fillets and a dash of red pepper flakes.

Heat olive oil in a skillet, then stir in the onion. Sauté 5 minutes, till tender. Stir in garlic and olives. Add tomatoes. Cook over medium heat, breaking up tomatoes, till boiling.

Simmer sauce uncovered, until slightly thickened (about 15 minutes). Stir in basil, salt, and pepper. Serve over hot, cooked pasta.

Garlic and Habañero Linguine with Olives

xxxxxx

Spicy but good!

Serves 4–5

Bring 6 quarts of salted water to a boil for the pasta.

In a separate skillet, heat oil over low heat. Stir in the garlic and cook 7–8 minutes until golden in color. Stir in the red pepper and sauté briskly about 1 minute.

Cook the linguine in boiling water until al dente. Drain, reserving ½ cup of the pasta water. Add the pasta to the skillet and toss with the garlic and oil, 6 olives, and the reserved pasta water. Sprinkle with parsley, season with salt and pepper, and garnish with remaining olives.

6 tablespoons olive oil

4–5 cloves garlic, thinly sliced

½ teaspoon crushed dried red pepper

1 pound linguine

6–12 habañero-stuffed or chili-flavored olives, pitted

2 tablespoons chopped Italian parsley

Salt

Coarsely ground pepper

Artichoke and Olive Marinara Pasta

xxxxx

Serves 4

The tangy addition of marinated artichoke hearts makes for a sauce that professional chefs call "bright."

2 garlic cloves, minced

¾ cup finely chopped onion

1½ tablespoons drained and minced bottled peperoncini

¼ cup olive oil

⅓ cup dry white wine

28 ounces Italian canned tomatoes with juice, chopped

2 jars (6 ounces each) marinated artichokes, drained well and halved lengthwise

½ cup chopped, pitted Kalamata olives

⅓ cup minced fresh parsley

Salt and freshly ground pepper

Sugar (optional)

1 pound penne or ziti pasta, cooked according to package directions

In a skillet, cook garlic, onion, and peperoncini in olive oil over low heat, stirring until onion is softened. Add wine and simmer for 4 minutes or until wine is almost evaporated. Add chopped tomatoes with juice and simmer 20 minutes. Stir in the artichokes and olives and simmer another 10 minutes. Add parsley, a dash of salt, and fresh pepper to taste. You can also add 1 teaspoon of sugar.

Serve hot over prepared pasta.

Olive Focaccia with Pancetta and Onion Topping

xxxxxx

Fast-rising yeast and a food processor make this bread a snap to prepare.

Makes 1 round loaf

1 3/4 cups (or more) bread flour

1 package fast-rising dry yeast

1 teaspoon sugar

3/4 teaspoon salt

3/4 cup hot water (125–130 degrees F)

2 1/2 tablespoons (or more) extra-virgin olive oil

1/2 cup chopped pitted Kalamata olives

1 tablespoon olive oil

2 ounces pancetta or bacon, chopped

1 medium onion, thinly sliced

1 1/2 teaspoons chopped fresh rosemary

Freshly ground black pepper

Fresh rosemary sprigs

Combine flour, yeast, sugar, and salt in food processor. Combine hot water and 2½ tablespoons olive oil in a cup. With machine running, slowly pour water mixture into processor through feed tube. Process until dough forms, then continue processing 40 seconds to knead. Add olives and process to combine.

Turn the dough out onto a lightly floured surface and knead until no longer sticky, adding more flour if necessary. Grease a medium bowl with olive oil. Add dough, turning to coat surface. Cover with towel and let dough rise in warm draft-free area until doubled in volume, about 35 minutes.

Preheat the oven to 375 degrees F. Grease a 13-inch pizza pan or baking sheet. Punch the dough down. Let it rest 5 minutes. Roll out on a floured surface to form a 12-inch round. Transfer to prepared pan and build up the edges slightly. Allow to rise in a warm draft-free area for 15 minutes.

Dimple surface of dough all over with fingertips and build up the edges again. Let rise in warm draft-free area for 15 minutes longer. As the dough continues to rise, heat 1 tablespoon olive oil in a heavy medium-size skillet over medium-high heat. Add the chopped pancetta or bacon, onion, and chopped rosemary, and sauté until onion just begins to soften slightly, about 5 minutes. Remove from heat.

Tilt the skillet with the onion mixture and, with a pastry brush, brush bread dough with olive oil from the bottom of the skillet, using additional oil if necessary to coat. Top bread dough with onion mixture. Sprinkle with freshly ground pepper.

Bake bread until brown on bottom and edges, about 30 minutes. Cut hot bread into wedges. Transfer wedges to platter. Garnish the focaccia with sprigs of fresh rosemary and serve.

Grilled Black Olive and Rosemary Focaccia
xxxxxx

Makes 2 round loaves

6 ounces water, heated to 105–115 degrees F

2³/₄ cups bread flour, plus more for kneading

1 package active dry yeast

¹/₄ teaspoon granulated sugar

¹/₂ teaspoon coarse salt, or to taste

Approximately 2 ounces extra-virgin olive oil, divided

¹/₄ cup cornmeal

24 Kalamata or Arbequino olives, pitted and halved

1 tablespoon chopped fresh rosemary

¹/₄ teaspoon freshly ground black pepper, or to taste

Salt

Although focaccia is traditionally baked in an oven, this recipe cooks on the upper shelf of a grill, allowing the bread to take on a hint of smoke flavor. Try it as an excellent accompaniment to Grilled Duck with Olives (see page 65).

Thoroughly combine the water, 1¾ cups of the flour, yeast, and sugar in a large bowl, or the bowl of a heavy-duty mixer fitted with a dough hook. Mix until smooth to form a sponge. Cover and let sit in a warm place for 45 minutes to 1 hour. The sponge should be thick, foamy, and bubbly, with a strong yeasty aroma. Blend in the remaining cup of flour and the salt. Turn out onto a floured surface and knead until a smooth, elastic dough is formed.

Shape the dough into a ball and rub it lightly with some of the olive oil, cover with a damp towel or plastic wrap, and let rise in a warm place for 1–2 hours, or until doubled in size. Punch down the dough and divide it into 2 equal pieces. Shape into rounds and allow it to rest while preparing the pans.

Lightly coat two 8-inch round cake pans with more olive oil and sprinkle generously with cornmeal. Gently tap out the excess.

Place a ball of dough in each pan. With your fingertips, push the dough out, working from the center, until it covers the pan. (If the dough sticks to your fingers, dip them in some olive oil.) Press the olives into the dough. Sprinkle with the rosemary and pepper. Cover the pans with a damp towel and let rise in a warm place until again doubled in size, about 45 minutes.

Preheat a grill to high heat. Place the pans on the upper shelf, cover the grill, and cook the focaccia until done. (Cooking time will vary according to your grill.) While still warm, brush generously with additional olive oil and sprinkle with salt. Cut into wedges and serve warm or at room temperature.

Elegant Entrées

xxxxxx

Grilled Porterhouse Steak with Olive and Caper Spread

xxxxxx

Do a really great steak justice with the highest-quality olives you can find!

In a food processor, coarsely chop the olives and capers. The olive and caper spread may be made 1 day in advance and kept covered and chilled.

Pat the steaks dry with paper towels, brush them with oil, and season them with salt and pepper. Grill the steaks on a rack set 4 inches over glowing coals for 10 minutes on each side for rare to medium-rare meat. (Alternatively, the steaks may be broiled on the rack of a broiler pan under a preheated broiler, about 4 inches from the heat, for 10 minutes on each side.)

Let the steaks stand, covered loosely with foil, for 8 minutes.

Serve the steaks sliced, with the olive and caper spread and parsley garnish on the side.

Serves 6

1 cup green olives (such as Picholine or Calabrese), pitted

1 cup black olives (such as Niçoise or Kalamata), pitted

1 tablespoon drained bottled capers

2 porterhouse steaks, 2 inches thick

Olive oil for brushing steaks

Salt and pepper

Parsley sprigs for garnish, if desired

Spicy Olive Burgers

xxxxxx

Serves 6–8

This recipe shows how even an ordinary hamburger can be literally transformed by the addition of olives.

2 pounds hamburger, shaped into 6–8 patties

6–8 slices pepper Jack cheese

Thousand Island dressing

6–8 onion rolls or kaiser rolls

2 fresh tomatoes, sliced

8-ounce jar of jalapeño-stuffed olives, sliced

Broil hamburger patties till cooked through, or grill to desired doneness on an outdoor grill. Place a slice of cheese on each patty. Return to broiler for 1 minute, or return to grill and cover until cheese is melted. Spread a dollop of Thousand Island dressing on the bottom half of each hamburger bun.

Place broiled patty first, then a tomato slice, and smother with sliced jalapeño olives and crown with the top half of the bun.

Veal Scaloppine with Green Olives

XXXXXX

Cremini mushrooms are a smaller cousin of the popular porto-bello variety. If you can't locate them at your local market, substitute sliced portobellos instead. Cracked Sicilian olives should be readily available at specialty food markets.

Bring salted pasta water to a boil and cook linguini for 8 minutes, to al dente. Drain and reserve, keeping warm.

Meanwhile, preheat a large, heavy skillet over medium to medium-high heat. Add 1 tablespoon of olive oil and the pancetta or bacon. Cook pancetta or bacon 1–2 minutes alone, then add onion and cook another 2–3 minutes. Add mushrooms and cook together with the onions for 3–5 minutes.

Season the veal strips with salt and pepper. In a second skillet, preheated over medium-high heat, add 3 tablespoons of olive oil and a smashed clove of garlic. Quick-fry half of the veal, searing each side of the strips for 1–2 minutes. Transfer cooked veal strips and garlic to a plate and repeat. Add all of the cooked strips and garlic to the onions and mushrooms, then add wine to deglaze the pan. Cook wine down to evaporate the alcohol, about 2–3 minutes.

Stir the olives and parsley into the veal and mushrooms. Serve portions of veal, mushrooms and green olives on a bed of hot linguini tossed with a drizzle of extra-virgin olive oil, butter and grated cheese.

Serves 4

$1/3$ pound linguini

Approximately $1/4$ cup extra-virgin olive oil, divided

3 slices pancetta or bacon, chopped

1 small onion, chopped

16 cremini or button mushrooms, chopped

1 pound veal scaloppine, cut into 1-inch strips

Salt and freshly ground black pepper

2 cloves garlic, smashed

1 cup dry white wine

16 pitted large green olives (preferably Sicilian), coarsely chopped

$3/4$ cup chopped flat-leaf Italian parsley

2 tablespoons butter, cut into pieces

$1/3$ cup grated Parmigiano-Reggiano or Romano cheese, a couple of handfuls

Pork Tenderloin with Olive and Corn Salsa

xxxxxx

Serves 4

The salsa makes this a real eye-catcher for dinner gatherings.

1 pork tenderloin (approximately 1 pound)

1 teaspoon chile powder, preferably chipotle

1 teaspoon garlic salt

1/2 teaspoon ground cumin

3 tablespoons olive oil

1 cup frozen corn kernels, thawed

1/2 cup pitted and sliced green olives

1/2 cup prepared salsa

1/4 cup chopped cilantro or sliced green onions

Slice the tenderloin across the grain into 1-inch filets. With a meat mallet or tenderizer, flatten slices into ½-inch-thick medallions. Rub thoroughly with the chile powder, garlic salt, and cumin.

Heat the oil in a skillet. Add the pork slices and cook over medium-high heat for 4 minutes per side or until no longer pink in the center. Transfer to a serving platter and keep warm. Add corn, olives, salsa, and cilantro to the skillet. Mix well and heat through, about 1 minute. Spoon over the pork and serve.

Halibut with Green Olives

xxxxxx

Serves 4

4 pounds halibut
fillet, skinned

Dash of lemon pepper

Flour for dusting

4 tablespoons
extra-virgin olive oil

1/2 cup dry white wine

3 medium tomatoes,
coarsely chopped

1 tablespoon spearmint

12 green olives

Serve this delicious fish dish with al dente pasta. The spearmint gives it a fresh spring flavor.

Cut the fish into large pieces. Season with lemon pepper and lightly dredge in flour, shaking off excess. Heat olive oil in a large skillet and add fish, cooking each side until lightly browned. Transfer fish to a warm plate and set aside.

Add wine to the skillet and boil for 3 minutes, stirring frequently. Add tomatoes, spearmint, and green olives, and cook for 4 minutes.

Place the fish on plates and top with the tomato sauce.

Lamb Meatballs with Black Olives

xxxxxx

For classic Greek flavor, serve these delectable meatballs with minted yogurt and lemony rice.

Place bread in a small bowl, cover with cool water, and soak for 5 minutes. Squeeze moisture from bread and place in a large mixing bowl. Add lamb, feta, olives, egg yolk, cumin, salt, pepper, thyme, and chopped bell pepper. Mix ingredients thoroughly. Take a small portion of the meat mixture, making a ball in your hand. Make 1-inch meatballs and set aside.

Heat olive oil in a large skillet. Place meatballs in skillet, turning occasionally until browned all over and thoroughly cooked. Transfer meatballs to paper towels and drain.

Serves 4 as an entrée or 8 as an appetizer

2 slices rustic Italian bread, crusts removed

2 pounds lean ground lamb

1/2 cup crumbled feta cheese

3/4 cup finely chopped pitted black olives

1 egg yolk

1/2 teaspoon ground cumin

1 teaspoon salt

1/2 teaspoon pepper

1/2 teaspoon thyme

1 tablespoon finely chopped red bell pepper

Lamb with Peppers, Potatoes, and Olives

xxxxxx

Serves 4

Rustic and warming, this is a great one-dish meal for cool weather.

2 tablespoons
extra-virgin olive oil

4 medium-size potatoes,
scrubbed, peeled, and
parboiled for 12
minutes, then sliced

5 green bell peppers, cored,
seeded, and cut into strips

1 1/2 pounds lamb
tenderloin, trimmed and
sliced

16 pink Arbequino
olives, pitted

1/4 tablespoon thyme

1/4 tablespoon oregano

1/8 tablespoon basil

1/2 teaspoon garlic salt

2 tablespoons
balsamic vinegar

Heat olive oil in a large skillet. Add potatoes and peppers and cook for 6 minutes, turning once. Add lamb, olives, thyme, oregano, basil, and garlic salt, and sauté for 8 minutes.

Add vinegar and cook over high heat for 2 minutes, stirring constantly. Add water if the mixture gets too dry. Serve hot with cooked rice or pasta.

Beef Stew with Black Olives

xxxxxx

A not-so-ordinary beef stew with a decidedly Mediterranean accent. Enjoy it with a glass of Merlot.

Heat a heavy-bottomed pan over high heat and sear beef in olive oil until brown on all sides. If pan is small, do this in batches rather than crowd the pan. Remove the meat and reserve, then add the carrots and onion to the pan and cook to soften. Return the meat to the pan along with garlic, thyme, bay leaves, orange zest, and red wine. Bring to a boil, and reduce liquid by a third. Add chopped tomatoes and olives. Cover with broth or water and simmer, partially covered, for approximately 2 hours.

Remove herbs and orange zest and taste for seasoning. Serve over soft polenta or noodles.

Serves 4

2 pounds beef stew meat, cut into 1-inch cubes

2 tablespoons olive oil

2 carrots, diced

1 onion, minced

3 cloves garlic, minced

2 sprigs fresh thyme

2 bay leaves

2 strips orange zest

1 cup Merlot or other red wine

1 cup chopped canned plum tomatoes

1/2 cup oil-cured black olives, pitted

1 cup beef broth or water

Polenta or noodles

Cheddar Olive Pie

xxxxxx

Serves 4–6

24-ounce package of frozen shredded hash brown potatoes, thawed

1/4 cup melted butter

4-ounce can green chiles, seeded and drained

1 cup grated Monterey Jack cheese

1 cup grated medium Cheddar cheese

1 cup sliced spicy green olives (chile-stuffed is good!)

1/2 cup milk or half-and-half

2 eggs

1/4 teaspoon salt

1/4 teaspoon pepper

I love recipes like this, simply because they work at any meal—breakfast, lunch, or dinner!

Preheat the oven to 425 degrees F. Press potatoes between paper towels to remove excess moisture. Press into a 9-inch pie pan to form crust. Brush with melted butter. Bake for 25 minutes or until crust rim is golden brown.

Spread chiles, cheeses, and olives evenly over the crust.

In a medium bowl, beat together milk, eggs, salt, and pepper. Pour mixture slowly into crust. Reduce oven temperature to 350 degrees F and continue to bake 30–40 minutes or until a knife inserted in the center comes out clean.

Braised Chicken and Olives

xxxxxx

Great for a crowd or a low-stress buffet.

Serves 8

Preheat oven to 325 degrees F. In a heavy dish suitable for both the stove top and the oven, and large enough to hold the chicken pieces in one layer, heat the oil over moderately high heat until it is hot but not smoking.

Pat the chicken dry and season with salt and pepper; brown in oil. Remove chicken to a plate and reduce heat to moderately low. Add onions to the pan and sauté until softened. Add garlic, bay leaves, thyme, and cumin, and cook for 1 minute, stirring.

Return the chicken to the casserole, along with any juices accumulated on the plate. Add olives and wine; bring to a boil. Braise the chicken, covered, in the oven for 20–25 minutes or until tender. Transfer the chicken and olives with a slotted spoon to a bed of hot cooked rice; cover loosely with foil to keep warm.

Boil the liquid in the pan, stirring occasionally, until it is reduced by half. Add the chicken broth and bring liquid back to a boil. Whisk in the dissolved cornstarch and boil for 1 minute. Strain the sauce through a fine sieve into a sauce boat. Drizzle some over the chicken and serve the remaining sauce separately.

2 tablespoons olive oil

4 pounds chicken, cut into serving pieces

Salt and pepper

2 onions, chopped

4 garlic cloves, minced

2 bay leaves

1 teaspoon thyme

2 teaspoons ground cumin

1 cup unpitted green olives

1 cup unpitted black olives

1 1/2 cups dry white wine

4 cups cooked rice

1 1/2 cups canned chicken broth

3 teaspoons cornstarch, dissolved in 1 tablespoon cold water

Chicken with Green Olives

xxxxxx

Serves 4

2 pounds chicken pieces

$1/_8$ cup lemon juice

$1/_2$ cup extra-virgin olive oil

$1/_2$ tablespoon thyme

$1/_4$ tablespoon basil

$1/_4$ tablespoon oregano

Dash of lemon pepper

$1/_4$ cup green olives

Another recipe for a marinated and braised chicken that goes the distance—great for simple family meals or a low-stress dinner party.

In a roasting pan, place chicken in one layer to fit.

Mix the lemon juice, olive oil, thyme, basil, oregano, and lemon pepper together. Pour the olive oil mixture over chicken, place chicken in refrigerator, and marinate for at least 1 hour, or longer as desired.

Preheat oven to 400 degrees F. Place chicken in oven and cook, uncovered, for 35 minutes, or until juices run clear.

Add green olives to chicken, distributing evenly, and cook an additional 10 minutes.

Turkey Cutlets with Capers, Olives, and Anchovies

xxxxxx

Serves 4

4 large skinless, boneless turkey cutlets, about 2 pounds

Flour

1/4 cup vegetable oil

1/4 cup olive oil

24 Gaeta olives, pitted

1 red bell pepper, julienned

3 tablespoons capers, drained

1/4 cup white wine

4 anchovies, drained and chopped

1/4 cup chicken stock

2 tablespoons chopped fresh parsley

1 tablespoon chopped fresh basil

Salt and pepper

Turkey cutlets have become readily available in most markets and make for a wonderful high-protein, low-fat change from the usual chicken.

Dredge the turkey breasts in flour. Heat vegetable oil in a large skillet. Brown cutlets quickly on both sides. Remove from pan and discard oil.

Add the olive oil to the pan, then add turkey, olives, bell pepper, and capers, and simmer 3–5 minutes. Add wine, anchovies, chicken stock, parsley, basil, and salt and pepper, and simmer, uncovered, until turkey is cooked through, about 5 minutes. Serve on a warm platter with rice or scalloped potatoes.

Grilled Duck with Olives

xxxxxx

A classic from French cuisine, with a twist for modern lifestyles. This recipe prepares the duck on an outdoor grill, for flawlessly crisp skin and added flavor.

Prick or score the skin of the duck all over. Grill the duckling plain and season it with salt and pepper as you turn it. Grill skin side up for 10 minutes, turn and grill an additional 15 minutes for medium well. Remove to a serving platter and keep warm.

In a saucepan over medium heat, melt butter until foaming. Add onion, white wine, olives, and more salt and pepper. Continue to simmer 5–10 minutes, or until the sauce is reduced by a third. Serve it over the duckling.

Serves 8

1 whole duckling, split

Salt and pepper

4 tablespoons butter

$1/4$ cup finely chopped onion

1 cup white wine

1 cup small green Spanish olives

Chicken, Olives, and Sausage

xxxxxx

A close cousin to the classic cacciatore, this recipe is ideal for a crowd of friends or a family gathering.

Preheat oven to 375 degrees F. Split and bruise 2 cloves of garlic and rub over the chicken. Sprinkle 2 tablespoons oil over the chicken. Add lemon juice, salt, pepper, and half the rosemary. Place the chicken in an ungreased baking pan and bake uncovered for 45 minutes (until juice runs clear).

Place sausage and 1 tablespoon oil in skillet and sauté 15–20 minutes. If your Italian sausage was in links, remove the skins now and slice the links into 2-inch pieces. Set aside.

When the chicken is done, chop remaining garlic and sauté until brown, about 1 minute. Add sausage and olives to oil. Cook 1 minute on high heat. Add tomatoes, remaining rosemary, and more salt and pepper. Sauté for 2 minutes. Stir in wine. Add butter and cheese and stir briskly until sauce becomes creamy. Pour over chicken and serve.

Serves 6–8

6 cloves garlic, divided

5 pounds chicken, cut up

Olive oil

Juice of 1 lemon

Salt and pepper

1 bunch rosemary, coarsely chopped

1 1/2 pounds sweet Italian sausage (either bulk or links)

1 cup Niçoise olives

8–10 plum tomatoes, seeded and cut into wedges lengthwise

Generous splash of red or white wine

2 tablespoons butter

3 tablespoons grated Parmesan cheese

Perfect Martinis
xxxxxx

Perfect Gin Martini

xxxxxx

What would a book about olives be without a recipe for the perfect martini? These elegant cocktails have probably done more for olives and their popularity than Athena herself.

Fill shaker and 2 martini glasses with cracked ice. Pour gin and vermouth into shaker. Shake or stir 10 times. Empty ice out of glasses. Strain martinis into chilled glasses and garnish with olives.

Serves 2

2 cups cracked ice

10 ounces gin

2 ounces dry vermouth

2 almond-stuffed olives

Perfect Vodka Martini

xxxxxx

Make sure to chill your glasses in the freezer first!

Shake or stir together all ingredients except for the olives. Pour into chilled martini glasses and garnish with olives.

Serves 2

$3/4$ cup cracked ice

$1 1/2$ ounces dry vermouth

$1 1/2$ ounces sweet vermouth

9 ounces vodka

4 martini olives

Dirty Martini

xxxxxx

Serves 2

Ice to fill shaker
1 ounce dry vermouth
9 ounces gin
1 ounce liquid from
a jar of olives
6–8 martini olives

For the best martinis, keep the gin (or vodka) in the freezer and the vermouth in the refrigerator to make your martinis extra-chilled and to keep the ice from melting too quickly.

Fill shaker with ice and add vermouth. Shake until ice is coated, then pour out vermouth Add gin and olive juice. Shake, then strain into highball glasses. Add olives and enjoy.

Southwest Vodka Martini

xxxxxx

Serves 2

½ ounce tequila
10 ounces chilled vodka
4 jalapeño-stuffed olives

Vary the flavor of your drinks with olives stuffed with different ingredients—jalapeño-stuffed work best in this recipe. Just remember, moderation is key—with liquor of course, not olives!

Swirl tequila to coat martini glasses, then pour out. Fill glasses with chilled vodka. Garnish with olives.

Salt-Cured Olives

xxxxxx

Yield varies with size and moisture of olives

8 pounds ripe black olives

5 pounds sea salt or coarse kosher salt

Olive oil

Garlic (optional)

Fresh thyme, rosemary, or other fresh herbs (optional)

Special equipment:

Wooden fruit crate or sturdy cardboard box

Burlap

This method produces the dark, wrinkled, and incredibly rich-tasting Greek-style olive, sometimes called "oiled-cured" olives. It's an excellent and time-tested method for curing olives in quantity—however, proportions can be adjusted for smaller amounts.

Cover the bottom of a wooden or cardboard box with burlap. Weigh out 1 pound of salt for each 2 pounds of olives. Mix the salt and olives well in the box to prevent mold from developing. Pour another layer of salt over the olives to a depth of 1 inch. Never place an airtight cover over curing olives.

After 1 week, pour olives and salt into another box, then back into the first box to mix them. Repeat this mixing process once every 3 days until the olives are cured and edible. This usually takes 30–35 days.

Remove the olives from the box with a colander or coarse sieve, sifting out most of the salt. Dip the olives momentarily in boiling water. Drain. Allow olives to then dry overnight, uncovered. The next day, cover with additional salt, using ¾ pound of salt for each 8 pounds of olives. Mix and put the olives in a cool place. Use within 1 month, or store in a refrigerator until needed.

Just before serving, using your hands, coat the olives with a fruity olive oil. If desired, mix with fresh flavorings of your choice, such as garlic, thyme, or rosemary.

Home-Cured Olives

XXXXXX

*Makes up to 1
gallon, depending
on how many olives
you start with*

Fresh-picked olives

Water

Kosher salt

1/2 cup balsamic vinegar

1 cup cider vinegar

If you're fortunate enough to live in an area where olive trees grow, you'll doubtless have noticed that every year, millions of olives go to waste simply because people don't know how to cure them. The truly dauntless olive-lovers among you will have no problem knocking on a stranger's door to ask if you might help yourself, or scoping out the local parks and municipal buildings for the chance to harvest the fresh fruit. Though most olives come to maturity in the autumn, olives can be picked at almost any stage once they are mature. The darker the olive, the more oil it has and the nuttier the flavor. Just make sure they are still firm and not soft and that all your olives are approximately the same size.

Rinse the olives, slash them, and place into a 1-gallon jar or crock. Cover with clear water and weight them to keep the olives under the water line (you can weight them with a clean plastic jug filled with water). Drain and change the water every day for 10 days.

After 10 days, cover the olives with a brine made of ½ cup coarse kosher salt per gallon of water. Once a week for 4 weeks, rinse the olives and cover with a new brine.

After 4 weeks, taste your olives for bitterness. Keep in mind that larger olives may take 2 or even 3 months before the bitterness is extracted.

Store olives in a brine solution made of ¼ cup kosher salt to 1 gallon of water, ½ cup balsamic vinegar, and 1 cup cider vinegar.

For safety, olives should be cured but not "canned" at home and should be kept refrigerated after curing.

Olive Pesto

xxxxxx

Something of a kitchen essential, olive pesto makes for an excellent condiment for all sorts of foods, such as pasta or fish. Or spread it over toasted bread for a quick, appetizing bruschetta. The recipe below is very basic, along with a couple of variations. Feel free to experiment—just keep in mind that your pesto will vary with the flavor of the olives you use.

Makes 1½ cups

1 large clove garlic

¼ teaspoon salt

⅓ cup piñon nuts

1 cup firmly packed, drained pimiento-stuffed green olives

1 cup minced parsley

¼ cup extra-virgin olive oil

4 tablespoons grated Romano cheese

In the workbowl of a food processor, mince the garlic with the salt to form a paste. Add piñon nuts, olives, and parsley. With the motor running, add the oil in a stream; then add the cheese and blend mixture well.

Store, covered, in the refrigerator for up to a month or in the freezer for up to a year.

Variations   For Black Olive Pesto, substitute 1 cup pitted salt-cured olives for the green olives; increase olive oil to ¾ cup and proceed as directed. For Southwest Pesto, using 1 cup salt-cured olives and ¾ cup of oil, add another clove of garlic and the following spices: 1 teaspoon chile powder, 1 teaspoon ground coriander, ½ teaspoon ground cumin, ½ cup chopped fresh Italian parsley, and ½ cup chopped fresh mint; proceed as directed in original recipe.

Harissa Morocco

xxxxx

Makes 1 pound

1 pound oil-cured black olives

1 teaspoon cumin seed

1/2 teaspoon coriander seeds

1/2 teaspoon caraway seeds

2 dried red chiles, stemmed but not seeded (about 2 inches in length)

2 cloves garlic

1/2 teaspoon coarse salt

1/2 cup roasted, drained, and chopped red bell peppers

1 tablespoon olive oil

1/2 cup additional olives

This indispensable North African condiment is wonderfully spicy, unusual, and exotic. It's often mixed with additional olives and served as an appetizer or with salads, couscous, or stews.

In a colander, rinse the pound of olives under cold water for 1 minute, then place them in a large bowl and cover them with cold water. Soak the olives 4 hours to remove excess salt, then drain them well.

Using a mortar and pestle, an electric spice grinder, or a cleaned coffee grinder, grind the seeds fine. If using mortar and pestle, add chiles, garlic, and salt to taste, and pound. If using a spice or coffee grinder, transfer seeds to a small food processor and add chiles, garlic, and salt. Grind mixture to a paste.

Add peppers and oil and pound or puree to a coarse paste.

To serve In a large bowl, stir together the harissa and additional olives, and marinate, covered and chilled, at least 6 hours or overnight. Serve at room temperature.